Pints, Quarts, and Gallons

Holly Karapetkova

Milk

1 Gallon

Juice

Juice

Ice Cream

Ice Cream

1 Quart

1 Pint

ROURKE PUBLISHING

Vero Beach, Florida 32964

www.rourkepublishing.com

PHOTO CREDITS: © Renee Brady: Title Page, 5, 8, 9; © Christopher P. Grant: 3; © tracy tucker: 7, 11, 19, 21, 22; © Kevin Thomas: 11, 13, 15, 18, 21, 23; © DNY59: 15, 17, 19, 20, 23

Editor: Meg Greve

Cover design by Nicola Stratford, bdpublishing.com

Interior Design by Heather Botto

Library of Congress Cataloging-in-Publication Data

Karapetkova, Holly.
 Pints, quarts, and gallons / Holly Karapetkova.
    p. cm. -- (Concepts)
 ISBN 978-1-60694-380-9 (hardcover)
 ISBN 978-1-60694-512-4 (softcover)
 ISBN 978-1-60694-570-4 (bilingual)
 1. Units of measurement--Juvenile literature. I. Title.
 QC90.6.K3685 2010
 530.8'1--dc22
                                    2009015992

Printed in the USA

CG/CG

Rourke Publishing

www.rourkepublishing.com - rourke@rourkepublishing.com
Post Office Box 643328 Vero Beach, Florida 32964

What is a pint?

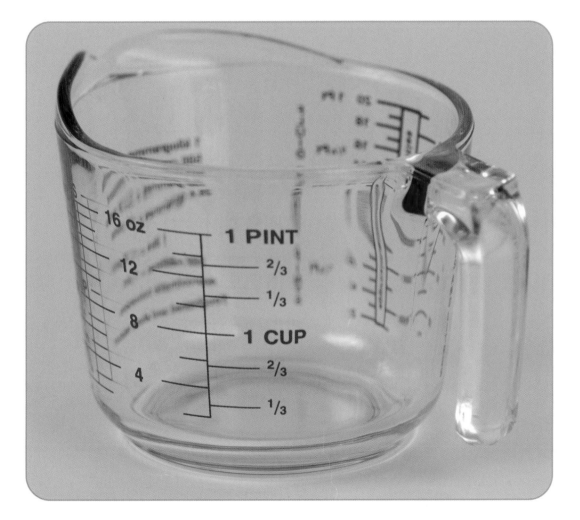

A pint measures amounts.
It tells us how much
we have.

Ice Cream

1 Pint

Juice

1 Pint

How much do we have?
We have one pint!

A quart also
measures amounts.

Ice Cream
1 Quart

Juice
1 Quart

There are two pints in one quart.

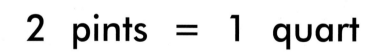

2 pints = 1 quart

2 pints

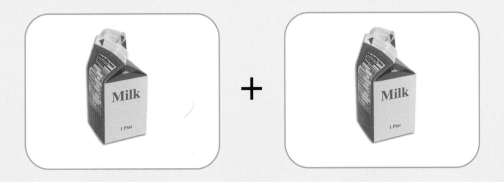

= 1 quart

How much do we have?
We have one quart!

There are four quarts in one gallon.

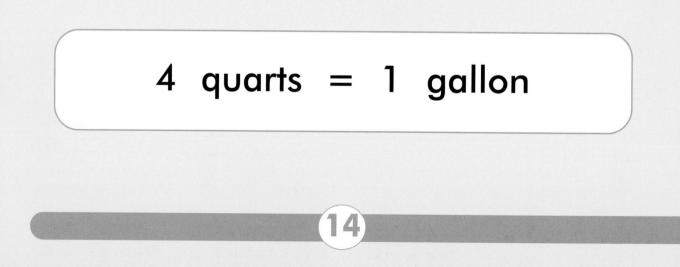

4 quarts = 1 gallon

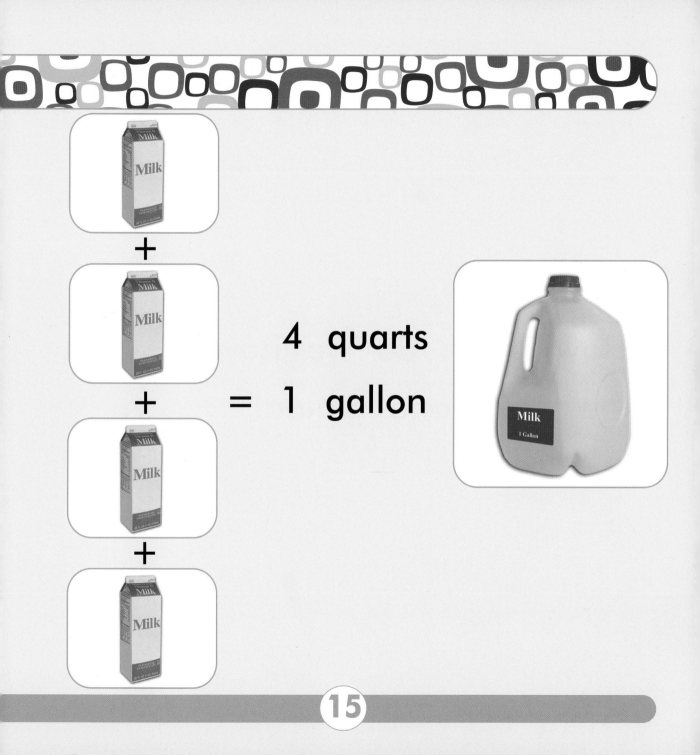

+

+

+

4 quarts

= 1 gallon

How much do we have?
We have one gallon!

Milk

1 Gallon

Which one holds the most?

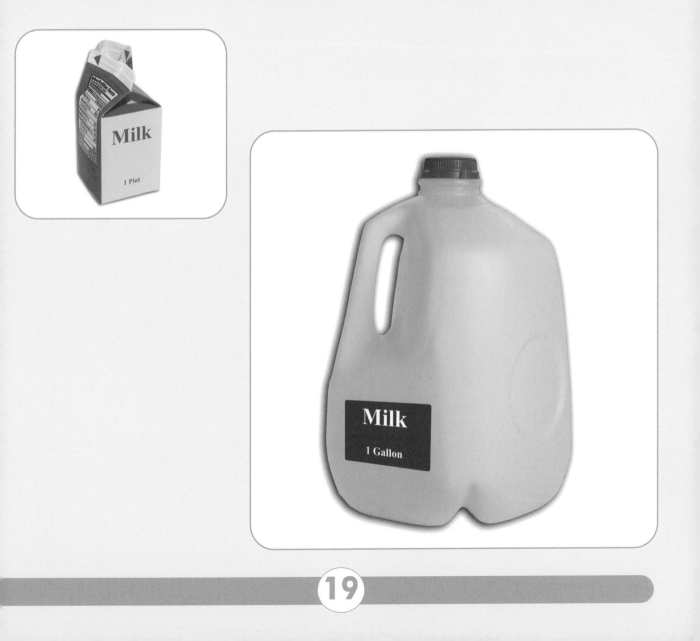

Milk
1 Pint

Milk
1 Gallon

Which one holds the least?

Converting Amounts from Customary to Metric

1 pint = 0.5 liter
(customary)   (metric)

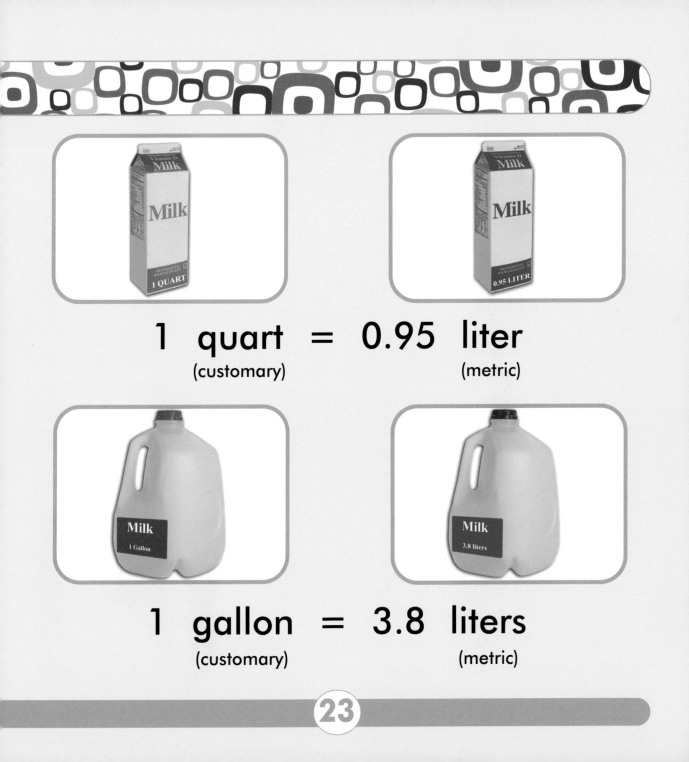

1 quart = 0.95 liter

(customary)   (metric)

1 gallon = 3.8 liters

(customary)   (metric)

Index

Websites to Visit

www.mathsisfun.com/measure/
www.edhelper.com/measurement.htm
www.factmonster.com/ipka/A0876863.html
pbskids.org/cyberchase/games/liquidvolume/liquidvolume.html
www.nzmaths.co.nz/volume-and-capacity-units-work

About the Author

Holly Karapetkova, Ph.D., loves writing books and poems for kids and adults. She teaches at Marymount University and lives in the Washington, D.C., area with her son K.J. and her two dogs, Muffy and Attila.

ML   1/10